History's Famous Friendships

John Adams and Thomas Jefferson

By Jill Keppeler

Gareth Stevens Publishing

Please visit our website, www.garethstevens.com. For a free color catalog of all our high-quality books, call toll free 1-800-542-2595 or fax 1-877-542-2596.

Library of Congress Cataloging-in-Publication Data

Names: Keppeler, Jill, author.
Title: John Adams and Thomas Jefferson / Jill Keppeler.
Description: New York : Gareth Stevens Publishing, [2022] | Series: History's famous friendships | Includes index.
Identifiers: LCCN 2020040325 (print) | LCCN 2020040326 (ebook) | ISBN 9781538264997 (library binding) | ISBN 9781538264973 (paperback) | ISBN 9781538264980 (set) | ISBN 9781538265000 (ebook)
Subjects: LCSH: Jefferson, Thomas, 1743-1826--Friends and associates--Juvenile literature. | Adams, John, 1735-1826--Friends and associates--Juvenile literature. | Founding Fathers of the United States--Juvenile literature. | Presidents--United States--Biography--Juvenile literature. | United States--Politics and government--1775-1783--Juvenile literature. | United States--Politics and government--1783-1809--Juvenile literature.
Classification: LCC E332.2 .K47 2022 (print) | LCC E332.2 (ebook) | DDC 973.3092/2--dc23
LC record available at https://lccn.loc.gov/2020040325
LC ebook record available at https://lccn.loc.gov/2020040326

First Edition

Published in 2022 by
Gareth Stevens Publishing
111 East 14th Street, Suite 349
New York, NY 10003

Designer: Katelyn E. Reynolds
Editor: Therese Shea

Photo credits: Cvr, pp. 1 (both), 5, 11 (main), 13, 22, 27 courtesy of the Library of Congress; cvr, pp. 1-32 (background) wawritto/Shutterstock.com; pp. 1-32 (frame) Olesia Misty/Shutterstock.com; cvr, pp. 1-32 (border) Vasya Kobelev/Shutterstock.com; pp. 7 (main), 15 courtesy of the Architect of the Capitol; p. 7 (Abigail) Mwanner/Wikipedia.org; p. 7 (John) Massachusetts Historical Society/http://www.masshist.org/database/40/Wikipedia.org; p. 9 (main) US Capitol/Wikipedia.org; p. 9 (inset) GraphicaArtis/Getty Images; p. 11 (inset) courtesy of the National Archives and Records Administration; p. 16 FPG/Archive Photos/Getty Images; p. 17 Leemage/Corbis via Getty Images; pp. 19, 21, 23, 25 Stock Montage/Getty Images; p. 24 duncan1890/iStock/Getty Images Plus; p. 28 (left) Barry Chin/The Boston Globe via Getty Images; p. 28 (right) littleny/iStock Editorial/Getty Images Plus.

Printed in the United States of America

CPSIA compliance information: Batch #CSGS22: For further information contact Gareth Stevens, New York, New York at 1-800-542-2595.

CONTENTS

*Words in the Glossary appear in **bold** type the first time they are used in the text.*

FOUNDING FRIENDS AND ENEMIES

They're sometimes called the "founding frenemies." That's because they were friends and enemies throughout their years as Founding Fathers of the United States. At different times, John Adams and Thomas Jefferson liked, respected, and even hated each other.

As leaders in the American colonies and the new country, these two men would both play major parts in the birth of the United States. From their meeting in 1775 to their deaths in 1826, their lives had a huge effect on the nation's beginnings.

MORE TO KNOW

BOTH ADAMS AND JEFFERSON ROSE TO BE PRESIDENT OF THE COUNTRY THEY HAD HELPED CREATE. ADAMS WAS THE SECOND PRESIDENT AND JEFFERSON WAS THE THIRD.

This picture shows John Adams at left and Thomas Jefferson at right. Founding Fathers Robert Morris and Alexander Hamilton are between them.

ADAMS BEFORE THE REVOLUTION

John Adams was born October 30, 1735, in Massachusetts. His father was a shoemaker and farmer. His family had lived in the American colonies a long time. He went to college at Harvard and taught school. He then went into law. He became well known among those who were against Great Britain's taxes on the colonies.

In 1774, Adams was elected to be a Massachusetts **representative** to the First **Continental Congress** in Philadelphia, Pennsylvania. One year later, he returned to the Second Continental Congress.

MORE TO KNOW

JOHN ADAMS WAS THE COUSIN OF SAMUEL ADAMS, ANOTHER OF THE FOUNDING FATHERS.

First Continental Congress

John Adams married Abigail Smith in 1764. The two wrote over 1,100 letters to each other. These give us a record of their thoughts on many subjects.

Abigail Adams

John Adams

JEFFERSON BEFORE THE REVOLUTION

Thomas Jefferson was born April 13, 1743, in Virginia. He was the son of a **surveyor**. He loved to learn. He spent a lot of time studying. Like Adams, Jefferson went to college. He then studied and practiced law. He became known as someone who knew a lot about the law.

In 1768, Jefferson went into **politics**. He was elected to the Virginia legislature, or lawmaking body. He supported American independence. In 1775, Virginia chose him as a representative to the Second Continental Congress.

MORE TO KNOW

STARTING IN 1768, THOMAS JEFFERSON BEGAN BUILDING HIS HOME, MONTICELLO, IN VIRGINIA. YOU CAN STILL VISIT IT TODAY.

Second Continental Congress

Thomas Jefferson

Jefferson was known as a shy and serious young man. He often spent 15 hours a day studying.

CHOSEN FOR THE DECLARATION

John Adams and Thomas Jefferson met for the first time at the Second Continental Congress. At first, the representatives said they were fighting for their rights as British citizens. Later, they decided to fight for independence from Great Britain.

In June 1776, the Congress picked five men to create a statement about why they were seeking freedom. Two were Adams and Jefferson. All five worked together on ideas for the statement. However, Adams asked Jefferson to write the **draft** of what would become the Declaration of Independence.

MORE TO KNOW

THE SECOND CONTINENTAL CONGRESS APPROVED THE DECLARATION OF INDEPENDENCE ON JULY 4, 1776. THIS DAY IS STILL CELEBRATED AS INDEPENDENCE DAY.

This picture shows (from left) Benjamin Franklin, John Adams, and Thomas Jefferson working on the Declaration of Independence.

IN CONGRESS, July 4, 1776.

Declaration of Independence

THE DIPLOMATS

After the Declaration of Independence, the colonies were at war with Great Britain for the next seven years. By 1783, they had won their freedom. The United States was officially its own country—with Adams and Jefferson as two of its Founding Fathers.

Both men were American **diplomats** in Europe during the 1780s. Adams lived in France and then Great Britain. Jefferson lived in France. They visited and worked with each other. Jefferson was welcomed into the Adams family.

MORE TO KNOW

JEFFERSON AND ABIGAIL ADAMS WROTE LETTERS TO EACH OTHER TOO. SHE TOLD A FRIEND THAT HE WAS "ONE OF THE CHOICE ONES OF THE EARTH."

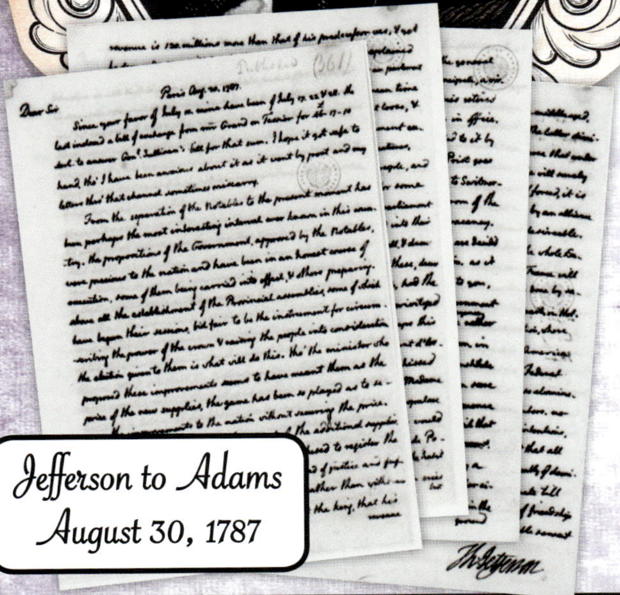

Jefferson to Adams
August 30, 1787

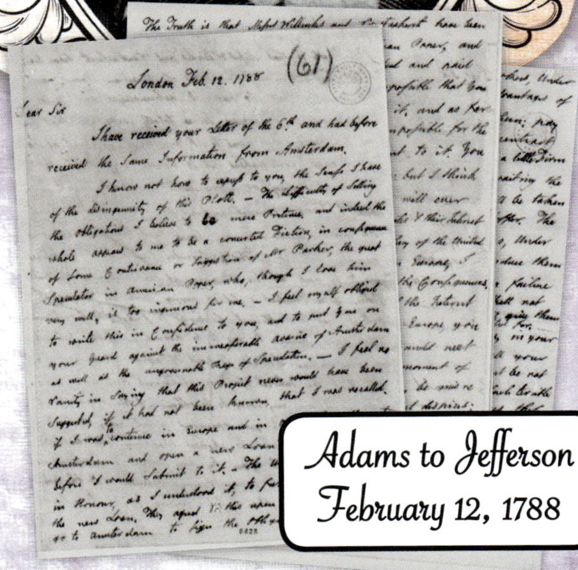

Adams to Jefferson
February 12, 1788

Jefferson and Adams wrote many letters back and forth. In one, Adams told Jefferson that this letter writing was "one of the most agreeable events in my life."

BACK AGAIN

John Adams returned to the United States first. In 1789, he was elected the first vice president, serving under President George Washington. At this time, the vice president was the second-place finisher in the election.

Jefferson returned to be in Washington's **cabinet**. As secretary of state, he was in charge of dealing with other countries. He hadn't been in the United States for the creation of the U.S. Constitution, the highest law in the nation. He had his own ideas about how the country should run.

MORE TO KNOW

THOMAS JEFFERSON DIDN'T LIKE THE IDEA OF A STRONG FEDERAL, OR NATIONAL, GOVERNMENT FOR THE UNITED STATES. JOHN ADAMS, HOWEVER, FAVORED A STRONG FEDERAL GOVERNMENT.

This picture shows George Washington, right, with his secretary of state, Thomas Jefferson (seated), and his secretary of the treasury, Alexander Hamilton.

DIFFERENCES OVER FRANCE

While they worked in the Washington **administration**, Adams and Jefferson's friendship started to come apart over their differences. Jefferson was a supporter of the French **Revolution**, which had started before he left France. He continued to support it even when it became more **violent**.

Jefferson didn't like that George Washington was neutral, or didn't take sides, toward the revolution. Jefferson left his role in the administration in 1793 and went home. Adams continued to support Washington and neutrality.

Washington's first cabinet

MORE TO KNOW

THE REIGN OF TERROR WAS A PART OF THE FRENCH REVOLUTION FROM SEPTEMBER 1793 TO JULY 1794. ABOUT 17,000 PEOPLE WERE KILLED BECAUSE THEY WERE BELIEVED TO BE AGAINST THE REVOLUTION.

The French Revolution took place from about 1787 to 1799. Many people died, including the king and queen of France.

PARTY TIME

George Washington served as president for two terms. He stepped down in 1796. Jefferson quickly returned to politics to run for the office. However, Adams ran for president too.

This election marked the first time that political parties played a part in a U.S. election. The Federalist Party supported a strong federal government. Adams was chosen as a Federalist **candidate**. Jefferson started the Democratic-Republican Party. Democratic-Republicans favored states' rights over a strong federal government. Jefferson was chosen as this party's candidate for president.

MORE TO KNOW

ALEXANDER HAMILTON WAS SECRETARY OF THE TREASURY. HE WAS IN CHARGE OF THE NATION'S FINANCES, OR MONEY MATTERS. THE DEMOCRATIC-REPUBLICANS WERE AGAINST HAMILTON'S FINANCIAL PLANS FOR THE UNITED STATES.

Though he never served as president, Alexander Hamilton was a powerful figure in early U.S. politics. He was one of the Founding Fathers who formed the Federalist Party.

PRESIDENT AND VICE PRESIDENT

When the election of 1796 was done, John Adams had won. Jefferson was a close second. That meant that he was Adams's vice president. Adams asked Jefferson if they could work together. He wanted to create a bipartisan administration, or a government that included both political parties.

Jefferson told Adams no. He didn't think he should work with Adams and be the head of the Democratic-Republicans. This caused a break between the two friends that wouldn't be mended for years.

MORE TO KNOW

IN 1804, THE TWELFTH **AMENDMENT** TO THE U.S. CONSTITUTION CHANGED THE WAY VICE PRESIDENTS WERE DECIDED IN THE UNITED STATES. IT CREATED SEPARATE VOTES FOR PRESIDENT AND VICE PRESIDENT.

Thomas Jefferson said he was against political parties. However, he created one and was the leader of it!

THE ELECTION OF 1800

By the election of 1800, Adams and Jefferson weren't friends. In fact, the election got mean. Jefferson started fake stories about Adams, including that Adams wanted to start a war.

The election was close again. However, it ended in a tie between Jefferson and another Democratic-Republican named Aaron Burr. That meant that the **House of Representatives** got to pick which man would be president. After many votes, they chose Jefferson. Before Adams left the presidency, he picked some of Jefferson's enemies for political positions.

Aaron Burr

MORE TO KNOW

ADAMS'S SUPPORTERS CALLED JEFFERSON "A MEAN-SPIRITED, LOW-LIVED FELLOW." JEFFERSON'S SUPPORTERS SAID ADAMS HAD A "HIDEOUS [UGLY] . . . CHARACTER."

Adams was unhappy about the election results. He left Washington, DC, without going to Jefferson's **inauguration**.

TWELVE YEARS OF SILENCE

After Jefferson took office, he and Adams wouldn't speak again for 12 years. The once-strong friendship seemed to be over. Jefferson served two terms, leaving office in 1809. Adams wrote a lot and saw his son John Quincy Adams rise in politics.

Benjamin Rush, a signer of the Declaration of Independence, was a friend of both men. He decided the men needed to talk again. He wrote to them. He told each that the other wanted to be friends once more.

John Quincy Adams

Benjamin Rush, shown, told both Adams and Jefferson that he had a dream that they were writing to each other again. It worked!

MORE TO KNOW

JOHN QUINCY ADAMS, JOHN AND ABIGAIL ADAMS'S OLDEST SON, BECAME THE SIXTH U.S. PRESIDENT. HE SERVED FROM 1825 TO 1829.

MANY LETTERS

Thanks to Rush, Adams and Jefferson started writing to each other again. Adams sent a note to Jefferson on January 1, 1812. Jefferson sent one back. They wrote 158 letters to each other over the next 14 years. They didn't always get along—but they wrote anyway.

The two men wrote about many things. They talked about the 1800 election and the French Revolution. They wrote about current events and about getting older. They even joked about their grandchildren and their great-grandchildren.

MORE TO KNOW

IN ONE LETTER, ADAMS WROTE TO JEFFERSON, "YOU AND I OUGHT NOT TO DIE BEFORE WE HAVE EXPLAINED OURSELVES TO EACH OTHER."

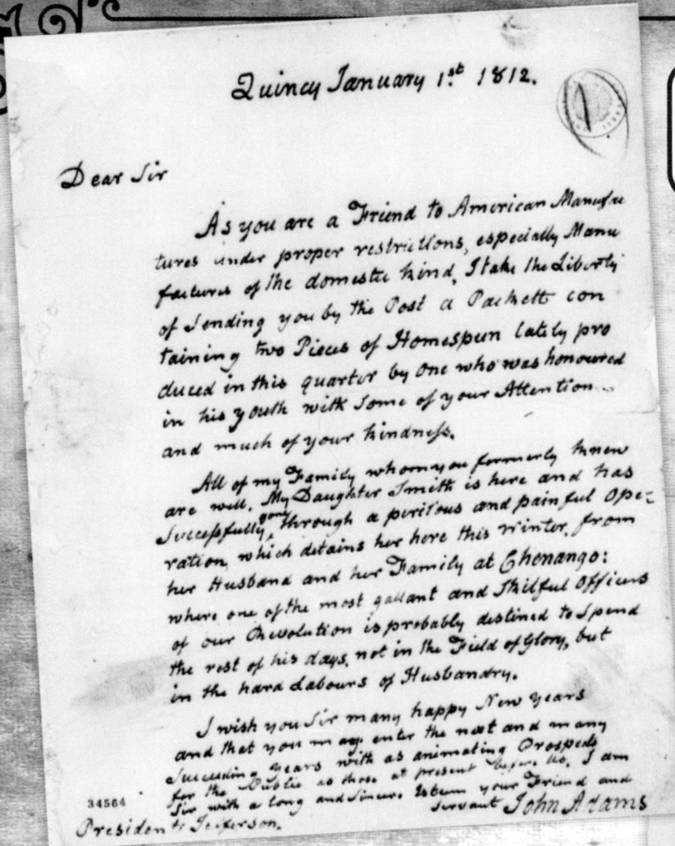

Quincy January 1st 1812.

Dear Sir

As you are a Friend to American Manufactures under proper restrictions, especially Manufactures of the domestic kind, I take the Liberty of Sending you by the Post a Packett containing two Pieces of Homespun lately produced in this quarter by One who was honoured in his youth with some of your Attention and much of your kindness.

All of my Family whom you formerly knew are well. My Daughter Smith is here and has gone through a perilous and painful Operation, Successfully, which detains her here this Winter, from her Husband and her Family at Chenango: where one of the most gallant and skillful Officers of our Revolution is probably destined to spend the rest of his days, not in the Field of Glory, but in the hard Labours of Husbandry.

I wish you Sir many happy New Years and that you may enter the next and many succeeding Years with as animating Prospects for the Public as those at present before Us. I am Sir with a long and sincere Esteem your Friend and Servant John Adams

34564

President Jefferson.

Adams to Jefferson
January 1, 1812

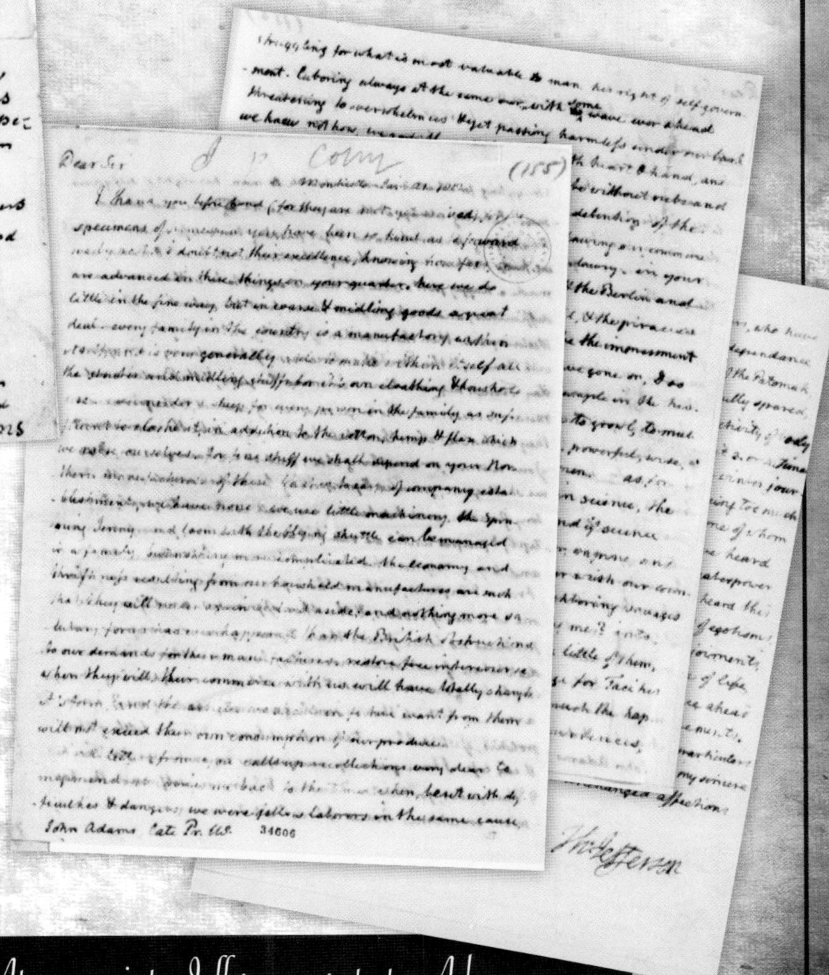

Dear Sir

I thank you before hand (for they are not yet arrived) for the specimens of homespun you have been so kind as to forward ... I doubt not their excellence, knowing how far you are advanced in these things in your quarter. here we do little in the fine way, but in coarse & midling goods a great deal.

Jefferson to Adams
January 21, 1812

Both men were growing old. At one point, Jefferson wrote to Adams that old "wrists and fingers make writing slow and laborious [hard work]."

ON THE SAME DAY

On July 4, 1826, the 50th anniversary of the Declaration of Independence's approval, 90-year-old John Adams became ill. His last words were about his friend Jefferson. Some report he said, "Thomas Jefferson survives." Others say he said, "Thomas Jefferson still lives." However, he was wrong. Jefferson had died earlier that day, at age 83.

Adams and Jefferson didn't always agree. However, they both wanted the best for their country, despite their differences. At the end of their lives, they were friends again at last.

Thomas Jefferson was buried at his home, Monticello. Adams was buried at a church in Quincy, Massachusetts.

An American Friendship

1735
John Adams is born on October 30.

1743
Thomas Jefferson is born on April 13.

1774
Adams is elected to the First Continental Congress.

1775
Adams and Jefferson meet at the Second Continental Congress.

1776
Adams and Jefferson are chosen to write the Declaration of Independence in June.

1776
Congress approves the Declaration of Independence on July 4.

1778
Adams is sent to Europe as a diplomat.

1783
The American Revolution officially ends.

1784
Jefferson joins Adams in Paris, France.

1789
Adams is elected the first vice president. Jefferson becomes the first secretary of state.

1796
Adams and Jefferson run for president. Adams wins. Jefferson becomes vice president.

1800
Adams and Jefferson run for president again. Jefferson wins.

1812
Adams first writes to Jefferson again. They exchange 158 letters over 14 years.

1826
Both Adams and Jefferson die on July 4.

GLOSSARY

administration: a government or part of a government that's identified with its leader

amendment: a change or addition to a constitution

cabinet: a group of senior officials appointed by the president as special advisors

candidate: a person who runs in an election

Continental Congress: a meeting of colonial representatives before, during, and after the American Revolution

diplomat: a person who is skilled at talks between nations

draft: a version of something, such as a document, that is made before the final version is made

House of Representatives: one part of Congress, which is the branch of the U.S. government that makes laws

inauguration: a ceremony marking the start of a term in public office

politics: the activities of the government and government officials

representative: a member of a lawmaking body who acts for voters

revolution: a movement to overthrow an established government

surveyor: one whose job is to measure land areas

violent: having to do with the use of force to harm someone

For More Information

Books

Barber, James. *Presidents*. New York, NY: Dorling Kindersley Pub., 2017.

Harris, Michael C. *What Is the Declaration of Independence?* New York, NY: Grosset & Dunlap, 2016.

Quirk, Anne. *The Good Fight: The Feuds of the Founding Fathers (and How They Shaped the Nation)*. New York, NY: Alfred A. Knopf, 2017.

Websites

Declaration of Independence: 1776
bensguide.gpo.gov/declaration-of-independence-1776
Learn more about the Declaration of Independence and what it means.

John Adams
kids.nationalgeographic.com/explore/history/us-presidents/john-adams/
See pictures and facts about the second president on this National Geographic Kids website.

Thomas Jefferson
www.timeforkids.com/g56/thomas-jefferson/
Learn more about the third president on this Time for Kids website.

Publisher's note to educators and parents: Our editors have carefully reviewed these websites to ensure that they are suitable for students. Many websites change frequently, however, and we cannot guarantee that a site's future contents will continue to meet our high standards of quality and educational value. Be advised that students should be closely supervised whenever they access the internet.

INDEX